CAVES

CAVES

by Stephen Kramer
photographs by Kenrick L. Day

NATURE IN ACTION

Lerner Publications Company • Minneapolis

To Grandma Bev and Grandma Ruth, and Grandma Bernice and Grandpa Milt

Many thanks to Dr. George W. Moore, Department of Geosciences at Oregon State University, and Charlie Larson, Western Speleological Survey, for their help with this book.

Text copyright © 1995 by Stephen Kramer
Diagrams copyright © by Lerner Publishing Group, Inc.
Photographs copyright © 1995 by Kenrick L. Day, except as credited on p. 48.

This book is available in two editions:
Library binding by Lerner Publications Company
  a division of Lerner Publishing Group, Inc.
Soft cover by First Avenue Editions
  an imprint of Lerner Publishing Group, Inc.
241 First Avenue North
Minneapolis, MN 55401 USA

For reading levels and more information, look up this title at www.lernerbooks.com.

Library of Congress Cataloging-in-Publication Data

Kramer, Stephen P.
  Caves / by Stephen Kramer : photographs by Kenrick L. Day.
    p. cm.—(Nature in action)
  Includes index.
  ISBN-13: 978–0–87614–447–3 (lib. bdg. : alk. paper)
  ISBN-10: 0–87614–447–4 (lib. bdg. : alk. paper)
  ISBN-13: 978–0–87614–896–9 (pbk. : alk. paper)
  ISBN-10: 0–87614–896–8 (pbk. : alk. paper)
  1. Caves—Juvenile literature. [1. Caves.] I. Day, Kenrick L., ill.
II. Title. III. Series: Nature in action (Minneapolis, Minn.)
GB601.2.K73 1995
551.4'47—dc20   93-42136

Manufactured in the United States of America
14-44247-6654-6/9/2017

Contents

Far below the earth's surface, water drips from the roof of a cave. The drops fall through darkness into a large stone room no one has ever seen. No bird has ever sung here. The scent of wildflowers has never hung in the air. For thousands of years, the tomblike silence has been broken only by the sound of falling water.

Drip.

Drip.

Drip.

Then, one day, footsteps break the stillness. Voices drift through the air. Flashlight beams cut across the darkness, lighting up a strange and wonderful sight. Stone icicles hang overhead. Smooth sheets of stone coat the walls. Huge pillars of rock connect the floor and the ceiling.

For the very first time, someone sees what the drops of water have made.

What Is a Cave?

A cave is a natural hole or passageway in the earth. The smallest caves are just big enough to hold one person. A large cave may have many miles of underground rooms and passages. Mammoth Cave, in Kentucky, is part of a cave system over 300 miles long.

Caves, sometimes called caverns, are some of the last wild, unmapped places on earth. They hold many secrets for explorers. Oddly shaped stones, hidden waterfalls, tiny plants, and strange animals are all found beneath the earth's surface.

Below left: A caver makes a discovery.

Below: A cave entrance high in the Rocky Mountains

People who explore caves are called cavers. When cavers discover a new cave, they try to answer certain questions: How large is the cave? How did it form? Do any animals live in it? Does the new cave have connections to other caves in the area?

Scientists who try to answer these kinds of questions are called speleologists (spee-lee-AH-luh-jists). This word comes from the Greek words for cave *(spelaion)* and knowledge *(logos)*.

Tackling a challenging cave

Types of Caves

Lava-Tube Caves

Caves are sometimes found in the layers of rock around volcanoes. When a volcano erupts, hot melted rock often pours out onto the earth. This rock, called lava, cools as it flows away from the volcano. As the surface of the lava cools, it may form a solid rock crust—like a pipe or tube—around the hotter lava inside.

When the volcano stops erupting, the hot lava may flow completely through the tube and out the other end, leaving behind a tunnel of solid rock. This tunnel is called a lava-tube cave.

Cavers explore a lava-tube cave in Arizona.

Sea Caves

Powerful ocean waves also can carve out caves. When waves crash against a cliff along the ocean shore, weak parts of the cliff slowly wear away. Eventually a cave forms at the base of the cliff. These caves are called sea caves.

Sea caves often contain calm, shallow pools that are homes for animals such as starfish and crabs. Some sea caves are also homes for seals and sea lions. They use the rocky ledges in sea caves as safe places to crawl out of the water and rest.

A sea cave on the Italian island of Capri. Sea caves provide quiet places for sea lions to nap *(right)*.

About 700 years ago, Native Americans called Anasazis (an-uh-SAH-zees) built homes inside sandstone caves in Arizona and Colorado.

Sandstone Caves

Millions of years ago, shallow seas covered areas of the earth that are now dry land. Over time, grains of sand on the bottom of the seas were pressed and cemented together into rock called sandstone. Later, forces deep in the earth pushed the rock upward, and the seas flowed away. Streams and rivers flowing across the sandstone slowly cut through it, forming canyons with high cliffs.

Moving water and wind sometimes work together to carve out caves in these cliffs. Day after day, week after week, water loosens the cement, and wind and water carry away the loose grains of sand. Over many years, a cave forms. This type of cave is called a sandstone cave.

Limestone Caves

Sandstone is not the only rock that formed in ancient seas. Countless tiny sea animals lived and swam in these seas. When they died, their shells and skeletons sank to the bottom. In some areas, the hard body parts of the animals formed thick layers. Over many years, the layers were pressed and cemented together by chemicals in the water to form a kind of rock called limestone.

The outline of a sea animal's shell can still be seen in this piece of limestone.

Then forces in the earth pushed the limestone upward, and it became dry land. Wind, flowing water, and plants slowly created a layer of soil on top of the rock.

In places like this, limestone caves may form. Limestone caves are the largest and deepest caves in the world. Many of them have long, twisting passageways, making them exciting to explore.

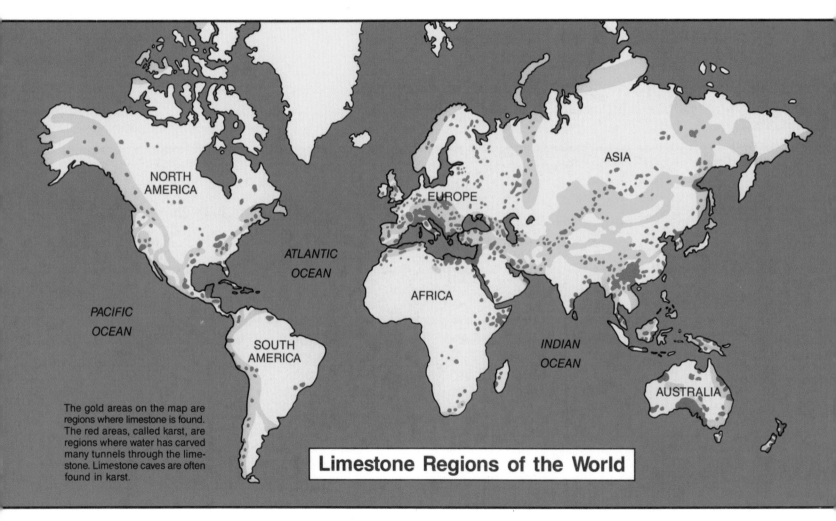

The gold areas on the map are regions where limestone is found. The red areas, called karst, are regions where water has carved many tunnels through the limestone. Limestone caves are often found in karst.

Limestone Regions of the World

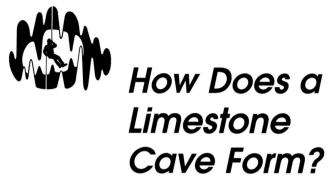

How Does a Limestone Cave Form?

Water and Carbon Dioxide

Dark clouds gather over limestone hills. A cool wind sweeps through the trees and down into the valley. Raindrops begin to fall.

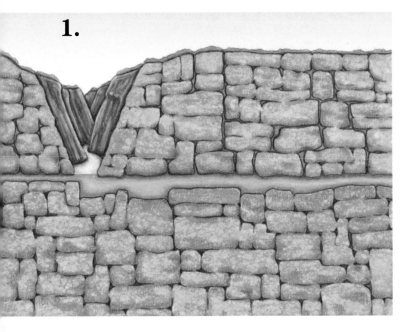

1.

As the raindrops trickle down into the earth, they pass through tiny air pockets in the soil. These air pockets contain a gas called carbon dioxide, which is given off by rotting plants.

When carbon dioxide mixes with water, the water changes into an acid called carbonic acid. The water does not look any different, but it is now strong enough to eat away limestone. If you put a small piece of limestone into a glass of carbonic acid, the limestone will slowly dissolve—in much the same way a spoonful of sugar disappears when you stir it into a glass of water.

The acid water seeps into small cracks in the limestone, and some of the rock dissolves (diagram 1). As time passes, the cracks grow larger and larger. Over many thousands of years, underground rooms and passages filled with water appear where there was once only rock.

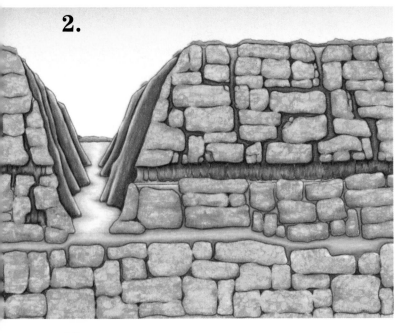

2.

A cave may remain filled with water for many years. Then, something changes. A nearby river carves a deeper channel, and the level of underground water drops. Or forces deep in the earth slowly push the limestone upward, causing the water to drain from the cave (diagram 2). The cave may still contain streams or ponds, but now much of it is dry. The cave stops growing.

A caver who understands how this type of cave formed can sometimes guess where it will lead. The cave will follow the path the water took as it traveled through the limestone toward the river.

Rainwater pours from a crack in limestone. It may have traveled underground for miles before returning to the surface.

Water and Hydrogen Sulfide

Not all limestone caves are formed by water trickling down from the earth's surface. Some are formed when water rises from deep inside the earth and mixes with a gas called hydrogen sulfide. This is the gas that gives rotten eggs their bad smell.

Water picks up hydrogen sulfide when it passes near pools of underground oil or pockets of natural gas. Together, water and hydrogen sulfide form an acid called sulfuric acid. When sulfuric acid rises through cracks in the earth, it dissolves some of the limestone in its path.

Limestone caves formed by sulfuric acid are especially exciting for explorers, because it is almost impossible to predict which way their twisting passageways will lead. A large branch of the cave may lead to a sudden dead end. A narrow passage may have an opening high on a wall that leads to another huge part of the cave.

In 1986, cavers discovered that an opening in a small cave on a rocky New Mexico hillside led to many miles of beautifully decorated rooms. The cave is named Lechuguilla (leh-chuh-GHEE-uh) Cave, for a spiny desert plant that grows in the area. During twelve expeditions, cavers mapped more than 50 miles of passageways carved by sulfuric acid. Scientists believe that the cave extends far beyond the areas that cavers have visited. It may be years before explorers reach the end of the passageways. Lechuguilla's neighbor, Carlsbad Cavern, is another remarkable limestone cave carved by sulfuric acid.

A caver rests at the edge of an underground lake in Lechuguilla Cave.

Speleothems

After the water has drained from a cave, another kind of growth may begin. Over the years, strange and beautiful stone shapes sprout from the ceilings and floors. Smooth, round stones appear in pools of water. Twisting stone fingers reach out from cave walls.

These remarkable cave decorations are called speleothems (SPEE-lee-oh-thems). Although they sometimes grow in lava-tube caves, sea caves, and sandstone caves, they are found most often in limestone caves.

Flowstone in Onandaga Caverns, Missouri

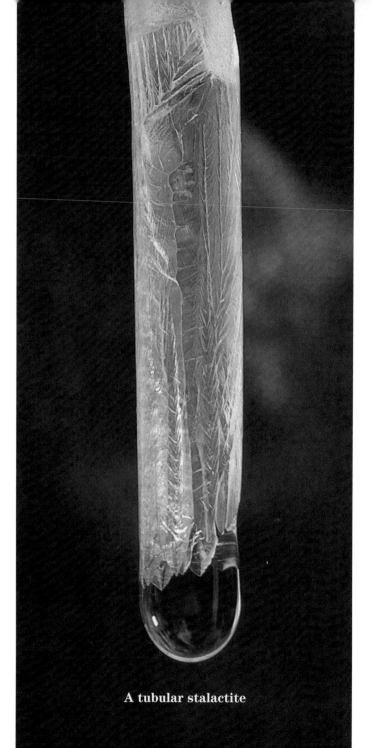

A tubular stalactite

Stalactites

A speleothem called a stalactite begins with a drop of water on a cave ceiling. The drop contains dissolved limestone that it picked up as it moved through the layers of rock above the cave.

As the drop hangs from the ceiling, a tiny amount of carbon dioxide from the water escapes into the air, just as bubbles of carbon dioxide escape when you open a can of soda pop. Now the drop cannot carry as much dissolved limestone. A tiny ring of stone forms around the outside edges of the drop. This stone is called dripstone. The drop of water hangs for a moment. Then it falls.

Each drop adds another layer as it trickles down through the growing ring of stone. Eventually the dripstone forms a slender tube that is long enough to see.

These hollow, slender stalactites are called tubular stalactites or soda-straw stalactites. They are very fragile. As they grow, their own weight may cause them to break off and fall to the floor.

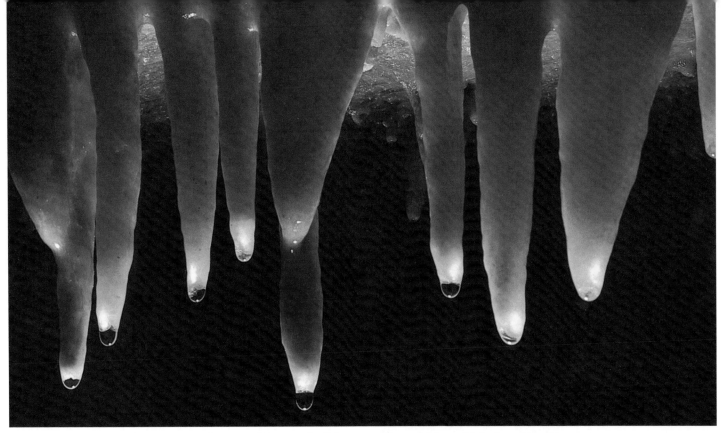

Conical stalactites are beginning to form as dripstone builds up on the outsides of tubular stalactites.

As the tubular stalactite grows, it often gets plugged with dripstone. When water can no longer flow down the inside of the stalactite, it flows down the outside. The flowing water leaves behind a very thin trail of dripstone. More of the dripstone is left near the upper end than the lower end, giving the stalactite the shape of a cone. This kind of stalactite is called a conical stalactite. Conical stalactites may also form when water seeping out of a crack in the ceiling flows down the outside of a tubular stalactite.

Stalactites do not grow very quickly. The fastest-growing stalactites are usually formed by fast-dripping water that contains a lot of carbon dioxide and dissolved rock. These stalactites might grow up to 12 inches in a hundred years. Most stalactites, however, grow much more slowly. On average, a stalactite grows only about 1/2 inch in a hundred years.

Stalagmites

Although a drop of water leaves dripstone behind when it falls from the ceiling, the water still contains some dissolved limestone. The dripping water carries this dissolved rock to the floor of the cave.

When a drop of water hits the floor, it spatters, breaking up into tiny droplets. At the same time, the water loses more carbon dioxide. Dripstone forms in the splashing droplets.

These two young stalagmites, *left*, are only about an inch tall. Thousands of years from now, they may look more like the huge ones above.

Speleothems with round, dome-shaped tops begin to form where the droplets land. These speleothems are called stalagmites. They can grow to be more than 45 feet tall and 30 feet wide. Like stalactites, stalagmites grow very slowly.

There is an easy way to remember the difference between a stalactite and a stalagmite. The word *stalactite* has a c, and it hangs from the ceiling. The word *stalagmite* has a g, and it grows upward from the ground.

Other Speleothems

Have you ever heard of cave popcorn? Or gypsum flowers? Cave pearls? Or moonmilk? These are names that cavers have given to some unusual speleothems they have discovered. Like stalactites and stalagmites, these stone decorations can be found in many limestone caves. New kinds of speleothems are still being discovered.

Sometimes a stalactite grows downward far enough to meet a stalagmite growing up from the floor. This kind of formation is called a column. As the water flows down the sides of the column, more layers of rock are added.

25

Below: Sometimes water enters a cave through a crack in the wall or floor. If the surface below the crack is smooth, the water may flow over it in a thin sheet. Layers of stone build up like icing on a cake. This kind of speleothem is called flowstone because the water creating it flows rather than drips into the cave. The flowstone-coated rock below, found in Carlsbad Cavern, is nicknamed "the Bashful Elephant." This elephant is only one foot tall.

Above: A drop of water that enters a cave with a sloped ceiling may flow along the ceiling from a high spot to a lower spot before it falls. As the drop moves, it leaves behind a trail of dripstone. Other drops follow the same trail. After many years, the layers of stone hang from the ceiling like folds of cloth. These speleothems, called cave draperies, are often less than an inch thick, but they may be several yards long.

Right: When dripping water carries dissolved limestone into a shallow pool of water, dripstone coats grains of sand or small pieces of rock lying on the bottom. These speleothems are called cave pearls because they look like smooth gray or white pearls made by oysters.

Below: These curving, twisted speleothems are called helictites. Most scientists believe that helictites form when water is forced into a cave through a very tiny opening in the ceiling, walls, or floor.

Left: Gypsum stalactites in the Chandelier Ballroom of Lechuguilla Cave. **Right:** Water running into a lava-tube cave during the winter in northern California created stalactites and columns made of ice—better known as icicles.

Some speleothems have smooth surfaces. Others are rough or prickly. They range in color from pure white to tan, yellow, orange, red, gray, or black. The differences are caused by the minerals that make up each speleothem.

When carbon dioxide escapes from water containing dissolved limestone, the dripstone that forms is usually made of calcite. Pure calcite stalactites and stalagmites are hard and white, and they have a smooth surface.

Sometimes, however, the dissolved limestone forms aragonite instead of calcite. Speleothems of aragonite often have sharp, pointed ends, and they look like white bushes. Like calcite, aragonite speleothems are hard.

Caves formed by sulfuric acid often contain speleothems made of gypsum. In Lechuguilla Cave, snowy white gypsum covers the walls and hangs from the ceiling like chandeliers. Gypsum is not as hard as calcite or aragonite, and it is usually found in dry caves.

Life in Caves

Cave Plants

Deep in the darkness of a cave, you will not find trees, grass, or ferns. Green plants make their own food using sunlight. This food gives them energy to make new leaves, grow flowers, and form seeds. The plants that live deep in caves cannot use sunlight for energy.

Bacteria and fungi (FUN-jie) are plants that grow well in caves because they do not need sunlight. These plants get energy from animal droppings, dead animals, or the leaves, stems, and twigs carried into a cave by a stream. Some bacteria can even make their own food by using the minerals found in caves.

The mushroom above sprouted up in bat droppings, or guano. The fungi on the right got their energy from owl pellets.

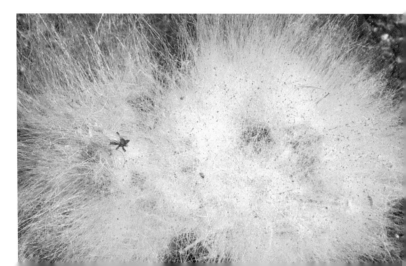

Right: This Chiapas cave crab, like many cave animals living in total darkness, is blind and nearly white.

Below: In parts of southern Europe, people used to think that caves were homes for dragons. They believed the white salamanders that sometimes washed out of caves were baby dragons.

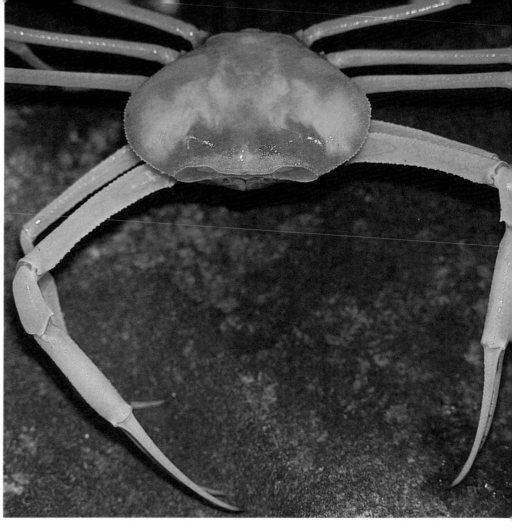

Cave Animals

Some kinds of animals spend their lives only in the dark parts of caves. They are called troglobites (TRAHG-lah-bites), from the Greek words *troglos* (cave) and *bios* (life). Certain kinds of fish, salamanders, insects, and spiders are troglobites. Being able to see is not important to troglobites, since they live in the dark. Many have small eyes or none at all. Instead, they usually have very well-developed senses of smell and touch.

Millions of Mexican free-tailed bats spend their summer days in caves throughout the southwestern United States. Their droppings, called guano, provide food energy for some kinds of cave plants and insects.

Other animals spend only parts of their lives in caves. They use caves for sleeping, staying warm during winter, or raising young. These animals are called trogloxenes (TRAH–gluck–zeens), from the Greek words *troglos* (cave) and *xenos* (guest). They are usually found near the entrances of caves.

The most well-known trogloxenes are bats. Caves are the perfect places for these night lovers to sleep through sunny days. During the summer, some caves in the southwestern United States are home to more than a million Mexican free-tailed bats. If you see these bats flying out of a cave at dusk, you may think you are looking at smoke from a large fire! When winter comes, some bats use caves as safe places to sleep away the winter. Other bats migrate to warmer areas.

31

A pair of bobcat kittens

Bears, raccoons, and bobcats are other cave guests. Charlie and Jo Larson will never forget the time they found bobcat kittens in a cave in southeastern Oregon. Charlie explains:

We were about 1,000 feet into the cave. In the darkness ahead, we heard what sounded like birds chirping. We couldn't imagine what was making the noise. Suddenly we rounded a corner, and there were five bobcat kittens. They must have thought we were their mother, because they came toward us. When they got close, however, they caught our scent and quickly backed up. We decided to turn around and leave too. We didn't want to disturb them—and we didn't especially want to be around when their mama came home!

Members of a third group of animals may live their entire lives in caves. However, these same kinds of animals can also be found under rocks, logs, or piles of leaves outside caves. These animals, called troglophiles (TRAHG-lah-files), like caves because they are moist and dark. Their name comes from the Greek words for "cave lover," and they include some kinds of salamanders and beetles.

A cave cricket *(top)* and a cave salamander *(bottom)*

This picture of a horse was painted about 15,000 years ago in Lascaux Cave, in France.

Humans and Caves

No one knows when humans first began exploring caves or using them for shelter. In caves near Beijing (also called Peking), China, scientists have found skeletons of early humans. These ancestors, called Peking People, lived about 500,000 years ago.

About 15,000 years ago, humans called Cro-Magnons explored caves in what are now the countries of France and Spain. These early people carried torches or stone lamps far into dark caves. There they painted animals such as bison, deer, cows, and horses on the walls and ceilings. Perhaps the artists hoped the paintings would bring them good luck in hunting. Or maybe they were keeping records of animals that they had already killed. No one knows for sure why these people hid their beautiful works of art so far underground.

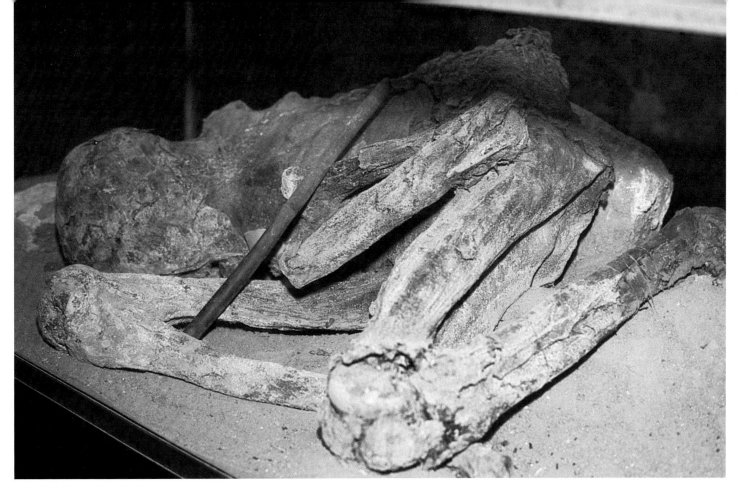

This mummy, called "Lost John," was a gypsum miner killed by falling rock in Mammoth Cave thousands of years ago.

As early as 4,000 years ago, Native Americans carried torches of dried reeds deep into Mammoth Cave, where they dug for minerals. These miners probably used gypsum to make white body paint. Other minerals may have been used to cure illnesses, season food, or call up spirits. Modern explorers have found gourds, shell spoons, and moccasins that these early explorers left behind.

Cave Safety

Traveling through a cave is often more difficult than traveling along the earth's surface. You may have to climb high rock walls or lower yourself down steep cliffs. You may have to cross underground rivers or lakes. And although cavers may be able to walk upright for long distances, eventually most of them have to get down on their hands and knees–or their bellies–to crawl through narrow passages.

Here are the rules cavers follow to help them stay safe:

Never enter a cave alone. If you twist your ankle or break your arm, there will be no one to help you or to go get help. Always have at least two other experienced cavers with you when you enter a cave.

Choose a cave that is right for you and your group. Some caves are level and easy to walk through. Others are more difficult, and cavers must use ropes and other rock-climbing equipment. Do not try to explore a cave that is too hard for the younger or less experienced members of your group.

Tell someone where you are going and when you plan to return. If an emergency happens and you cannot get out of the cave, someone needs to send help.

Be sure you have the equipment you need to travel safely. Your life may depend on the clothing and equipment you use underground. Most of a caver's supplies are the same ones you would carry on a backpacking trip: food,

This teenage girl knows how to use mountain-climbing equipment to rappel into a cave. For a younger or less experienced caver, the cave might be too difficult.

water, a rope, a map of the cave, and a small first-aid kit. In addition, there are three things every caver needs:

- Strong, durable clothing and shoes
- A sturdy rock-climbing helmet with a chin strap
- A good source of light and two backup lights. Most cavers have one light attached to their helmet and bring flashlights or candles as backups.

Remember that cavers sometimes spend more time in a cave than they had planned. Pack a little more food than you think you'll need. Also, carry along something to produce heat, such as a candle or small stove.

Books like this can help you understand some of the rules for staying safe in a cave. But books are only a start. Traveling with an experienced caver is the best way to learn about cave safety. For the names of caving groups in your area, send a self-addressed, stamped envelope to:

National Speleological Society
2813 Cave Avenue
Huntsville, AL 35810

Some of the items a caver might carry in a pack:
1. bottles of water
2. a small stove
3. spare parts for a carbide headlamp
4. candles and matches (in a waterproof container)
5. a hand line, used as a handrail in slippery or narrow passages
6. a caver sling, clipped to a rope and placed around the hips or chest for extra support or safety
7. a flashlight with extra batteries
8. Prusik slings, short looped and knotted ropes that can be attached to a longer rope to form a ladder
9. a first-aid kit

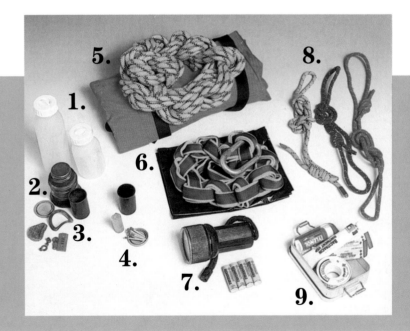

 # *Protecting Caves*

When you sit quietly in a cave, surrounded on all sides by solid rock, time seems to stand still. The air is so quiet you can hear your heart beat. Drops of falling water whisper in the darkness, just as they have for thousands of years. It's easy to believe that nothing about the cave will ever change.

But caves, and the plants and animals that live in them, are fragile. Like other wilderness areas, they need protection.

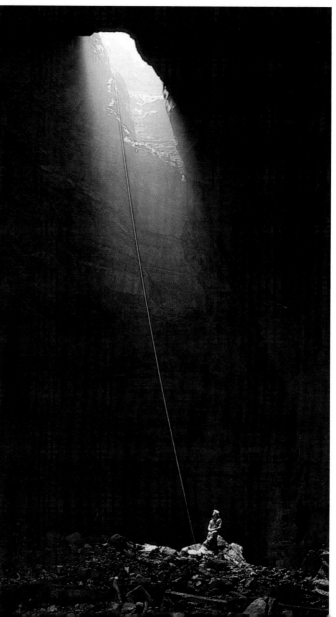

Caves can be harmed by things that happen on the earth's surface. Polluted water can carry sewage and chemicals from factories or farms into caves. Dams can cause lakes or rivers to rise, filling nearby caves. Animals living in these caves may drown. Speleothems stop growing. The caves can no longer be visited or studied.

Most cave damage, however, is done by careless or thoughtless visitors. Some people dump their trash in caves. Others paint cave walls, carve their names on rocks, or break speleothems. In a few seconds, vandals can destroy the beauty of a cave that took hundreds of thousands of years to form.

Above: Careless cavers broke many of these stalactites.

Left: Vandals have painted graffiti on the walls of this lava-tube cave.

39

Cavers who understand the importance of preserving caves have developed a motto: *Cave softly.* They try to explore caves so carefully that no one will be able to tell they have passed through. In a cave, a single careless arm movement can break a stalactite. One wrong step can destroy a stalagmite. In a narrow passageway, a careless head movement can shatter a dozen or more twisting helictites.

Cavers sometimes practice movements they need to use inside caves. They set up obstacle courses and practice crawling around, over, and under objects. Practicing these movements helps them learn how to travel through caves without damaging speleothems.

Cavers sometimes set up obstacle courses in boxes like this to practice crawling through tight passages.

By caving softly, visitors help make sure that a cave will be just as beautiful next week, next month, or years from now. Here are some suggestions for caving softly:

Always get permission. Before you enter a cave, check with the person or government agency in charge of it.

Respect the wildlife. Find out what kinds of animals use the cave before you enter it, and be careful not to bother them. It is especially important not to awaken hibernating bats, because they will use up energy that is supposed to help them survive until spring.

Stay on paths. Cavers have often marked the best paths to follow. If you stay on these paths, you will not damage speleothems or leave stray footprints.

Do not make any permanent marks. If you need markers to help you find your way back, cave softly by using plastic flags or something else you can easily pick up on your way out.

Do not touch speleothems. A dirty hand can leave muddy fingerprints. Even a clean hand can leave oils behind that may stop or change a speleothem's growth.

Above: A path marked with stones

Below: The person on the left is not caving softly. Can you see why?

Do not take any cave souvenirs. All speleothems, even broken ones, should be left where they are. If you find bones, fossils, arrowheads, or other ancient materials, leave them alone. Many states have laws protecting the contents of caves. When you leave the cave, tell someone in the science or anthropology department of the nearest college or university what you found.

Leave a cave better than you found it. Be sure to remove everything that you take into a cave. If you find any litter that other visitors have left behind, take that out with you too.

Using a long hose, this man is cleaning handprints and footprints off of speleothems.

Beneath the surface of the earth lie some of our planet's last unexplored places. By sharing what you know about caves with others, and remembering to cave softly, you can help preserve the wildness and beauty of these remarkable underground treasures.

Fascinating Facts

Slaves traveling to freedom along the Underground Railroad were often sheltered in caves. According to local legend, Meramec Caverns, in Missouri, was used to hide runaway slaves. Years later, in the 1940s, Meramec Caverns became one of several caves used as a fallout shelter—a place for people to go if an atomic bomb exploded.

Carlsbad Cavern was discovered in 1901 by a cowboy named Jim White, who was searching for lost cattle on a New Mexico ranch. One evening as the sun was setting, he saw what he thought was a column of smoke rising from a spot in the hills. When he later explored the area, he discovered that the "smoke" that rose into the sky was a stream of millions of bats coming out of a hole in the ground.

It's easy to see how Jim White mistook a swarm of bats for smoke.

In Scandinavian countries, people once believed that caves were homes for trolls. They thought that trolls dug in the ground to find precious stones. People also thought you could get rid of trolls by getting them to come out in the sunlight, where they would either burst or turn to stone.

In 1842, Mammoth Cave was used to house patients with tuberculosis, an easily spread disease. Several patients in the cave claimed they had been cured there, but after two patients died, the hospital was closed.

Ruins of a tuberculosis patient's quarters in Mammoth Cave.

Glowworms glisten on the ceiling of Waitomo Cave, in New Zealand.

Glowworms live on the walls and ceilings of some caves in Australia and New Zealand. They capture flying insects by dangling sticky silk threads into the darkness. When insects fly toward the glowworms' light, they get caught in the threads. The glowworms then pull up the threads and eat the insects.

# Glossary

Carbonic acid: An acid formed when water mixes with carbon dioxide gas. It can dissolve limestone.

Cave: A natural space under the earth's surface that is large enough to hold a person. Another name for a cave is *cavern*.

Cave drapery: A rock formation that hangs from a cave ceiling like a curtain or drapery

Cave pearl: A smooth, round rock formation found in some shallow pools of water in caves

Caver: A person who explores caves. Another name for a caver is *spelunker*, but most cave explorers prefer to be called cavers.

Column: A rock formation created when a stalactite and a stalagmite grow together

Dripstone: The stone left behind when carbon dioxide gas escapes from dripping or splashing water carrying dissolved limestone

Flowstone: The stone left behind when carbon dioxide gas escapes from flowing water carrying dissolved limestone

Helictite: A delicate, twisted rock formation that grows on a cave ceiling, wall, or floor

Lava-tube cave: A type of cave formed near a volcano when the surface of hot lava cools and the melted rock inside flows away

Limestone: A type of rock formed from the skeletons and shells of tiny creatures that lived in the sea long ago

Limestone cave: A type of cave formed when carbonic or sulfuric acid dissolves limestone and carries it away

Sandstone cave: A type of cave formed when water and wind loosen and carry away sand from a sandstone cliff

Sea cave: A type of cave formed when the force of ocean waves wears away rock at the base of a sea cliff

Speleologist: A scientist who studies caves

Speleothem: A rock formation such as a stalactite or stalagmite that is created when water deposits minerals in a cave

Stalactite: A rock formation that hangs from the ceiling of a cave. A stalactite begins as a narrow tube of dripstone called a tubular stalactite. If it becomes plugged, it develops a cone shape and is called a conical stalactite.

Stalagmite: A rock formation created when dripping water deposits minerals on a cave floor

Sulfuric acid: An acid formed when underground water mixes with hydrogen sulfide gas. It can dissolve limestone.

Troglobite: Any type of animal that lives only in the dark areas of caves

Troglophile: Any type of animal that can spend its life in dark parts of caves, but can also live its entire life in moist, dark places outside caves

Trogloxene: Any type of animal that lives above ground, but moves into caves to sleep, spend the winter, or raise its young

METRIC CONVERSION CHART		
To find measurements that are almost equal		
WHEN YOU KNOW:	MULTIPLY BY:	TO FIND:
inches	2.54	centimeters
feet	30.48	centimeters
yards	0.91	meters
miles	1.61	kilometers

Index

Additional photos courtesy of: © Kent & Donna Dannen, pp. 17, 35; © Russ Finley, p. 26 (right); © Michael H. Francis, p. 11 (right); French Government Tourism Office, p. 34; © Earl. L. Kubis/Root Resources, p. 33 (top); © Charlie & Jo Larson, p. 32; Library of Congress, p. 30 (left); David & Janet McClurg, pp. 36, 37, 39 (right), 40; © Robert & Linda Mitchell, pp. 29 (both), 30 (right); Eda Rogers/Sea Images, p. 13; © Pat Troops, p. 41 (bottom); © Merlin D. Tuttle, pp. 31, 44; Waitomo Caves Musuem, p. 45 (right); Kentucky Library/Western Kentucky University, p. 45 (left); and © Bob Zehring, p. 11 (left). Illustrations on pages 14 and 16 by Laura Westlund.